REACH OUT

C

F

OUTSIDE

LAURA TRENEER

BRF

The Bible Reading Fellowship
15 The Chambers, Vineyard
Abingdon OX14 3FE
brf.org.uk

The Bible Reading Fellowship (BRF) is a Registered Charity (233280)

ISBN 978 0 85746 553 5
First published 2017
10 9 8 7 6 5 4 3 2 1 0
All rights reserved

Text © Laura Treneer 2017
This edition © The Bible Reading Fellowship 2017

The author asserts the moral right to be identified as the author
of this work

Acknowledgements

Scripture quotations are taken from The Holy Bible, New
International Version (Anglicised edition) copyright © 1979, 1984,
2011 by Biblica. Used by permission of Hodder & Stoughton
Publishers, an Hachette UK company. All rights reserved. 'NIV' is a
registered trademark of Biblica. UK trademark number 1448790

Cartoon reproduced under licence and by kind permission of Dave
Walker/www.cartoonchurch.com

Every effort has been made to trace and contact copyright owners
for material used in this resource. We apologise for any inadvertent
omissions or errors, and would ask those concerned to contact us
so that full acknowledgement can be made in the future.

A catalogue record for this book is available from the British Library

Printed and bound in the UK by Zenith Media NP4 0DQ

Contents

Introduction

If the majority of UK adults never really go into a church, or if they do only for a 'special service' like a wedding, funeral or carols, then how do churches speak to them in homes, shops and neighbourhoods? If we say that church is about the people not the building, then how does the church incarnate communicate at times other than 10.30 to 12.00 on a Sunday?

This series of books starts with the understanding that it is primarily and ultimately God who communicates. He's equipped us to take part. There may be times when our churches feel like invisible pods on Planet 'Unchurched', but God's Spirit is at work around us among our friends and neighbours, whether or not they ever come to church.

In numerous ways you may not ever notice, your church already communicates outside its building. I hope this resource will reveal these, and point to other ways the church could do this with more intention, perhaps more vision, certainly more commission. 'External comms' as they could be called, carefully and cohesively combined with 'internal comms', 'digital comms' and wel comms(!), are a powerful mix, enough to make even the most invisible visible. And God makes the impossible possible… a combination worth working for.

If, however, everything that happens outside the building is disconnected from the inside and from your website and social media, there is a risk of communicating little more than an identity crisis.

One night in London, someone broke into St Mary's, Newington, not to steal anything, but to light all the candles and pray. As the priest wrote in *The Guardian* afterwards, their evident desire for 'silence and time' was understandable: 'In this fantasy-busting environment [of church] I am lent the courage to open the most defended bits of me to the infinite love of God… The need for God can be just too strong, overwhelming. And I totally get why someone might break into a church to find it.'[1]

They saw the building and it spoke to them so much of God that they had to get inside. There is something about the physical space enclosed by a church, the presence of it, the immovability of it, that speaks powerfully: Prayer. God. Him, not me.

Acts 16 talks about a 'place of prayer': 'we went outside the city gate to the river, where we expected to find a place of prayer… Once when we were going to the place of prayer, we were met by a female slave'.[2] This wasn't necessarily a building, but it was a physical place, a marker, where those seeking God went in expectation, and where encounters of transformation took place. They expected to find a place of prayer. Someone had told them it was there. They had been alert to its presence—and *awareness* turned to *interest*, to *desire*, to *action*, the four-stage process (summarised as AIDA) that companies use to track our internal journey.

Are people in your community *aware* of your church? Would they think of it as a place of prayer? Are you communicating enough to pique their *interest*? If this interest turns into *desire*, for church, for God or for both, do they have enough information to take *action*? One thing has been proven again and again: when awareness and interest dip, desire and action are unlikely.

Churches have an immense opportunity! Not only do they get to be places of sacramental worship, teaching, communion, fellowship and all those other things that are understood by most UK Christians, but not necessarily by their neighbours. They also get to be lights in their community and centres of communication about what it is to be a follower of Christ. Churches get to ask the big questions in the public sphere: to provoke, stimulate and challenge. Through every means of communication we have available to us—buildings, services, ministries, websites, printed invites, social media, videos, magazines, news-sheets, noticeboards, the smiles on our faces, the words from our mouths—churches can fundamentally change perceptions of Jesus Christ and those who believe he still has the power to change lives.

This series is for those who feel responsibility for church communications, and for those who think they make a difference.

The options can seem overwhelming—but time, budget and, let's face it, imagination, can be limited. I hope the tools in these books will help you form a simple strategy and plan that starts squarely in the reality of your situation. It's written so that the intimidated can relax and the goal-oriented can focus.

1

Why it matters

I know why it matters, you might say! Why else would I be reading a book on church communication? If so, would you justify improving the communications inside your church for the following three reasons? If not, do they convince you?

Because local communities need local churches

I remember hearing Bill Hybels from Willow Creek Church in the US saying that 'the local church is the hope of the world'. It is one of his mantras, memorable not least because it juxtaposes what is often perceived as weak (we hear 'local church' and we think of our own) with the immense, eternal purposes of God. Perhaps he was inspired by the great British preacher Charles Spurgeon who, in 1863, proclaimed this in the centre of London: 'The Church is the world's hope! As Christ is the hope of the Church, so the Church is the hope of the world!'[3]

Spurgeon was speaking in a context where, as he says, 'You went home this morning and you saw people in their shirt-sleeves lolling about and waiting at the corner till the bars opened that they might go in and drink. And you will go home tonight and see what you do not like to see.' He asks the question: are there times when we wonder why we can't all just go straight to heaven? His answer? 'It is just possible that you are put there for some end or design! Who can tell the benefit your good example may be?'

Local churches are the hope of the world because they are the bride of Christ incarnate in local communities. Sure, God knows why he's put us there of all places, but he's got a reason. As comedian Milton Jones says, if the church is the bride of Christ, she must have a lovely personality. By being on our street we are a standing witness to Christ. By being a Christian on your street you are influencing others. Your light is shining, even if you're hiding it sometimes. There are wonderful churches all over the world and many Christians present online too, but people live in physical homes (normally), on a street, in a town, city or village. We cannot be anything but local. Spurgeon has more advice, so uncannily prescient to the external communications of a modern church that it's worth reproducing:

You did not get into these places of your own choice, but if God [has done it], do not be in a hurry to undo it… if God has placed you there, be like Paul—be very prudent. Do not talk very much. There is wisdom in holding your tongue. If you are placed in a family that is irreligious, make them value you—show them that you will do anything you can to serve them. They will not believe in the reality of your spiritual affection unless you show a temporal affection, too. And when the time comes, do not hesitate to speak, but let your speaking be mainly by your actions!

Do not conceal your godliness from those around you! Though at first they may laugh at you and despise you, who can tell but that, like Paul, you may gain influence till they will do anything you tell them? And like Paul, by means of that influence, you may save all that are in the house and so the text may come true of you, 'God has given you all them that sail with you.'

As Spurgeon said, our neighbours are the family in which we have been placed. Even if they don't realise they need us, we may already be offering to meet some of their physical need (a place of community), and are certainly offering to meet their spiritual need (a place of prayer). A YouGov poll suggested that 47% of people agreed that the church was there for everyone. Now we need to communicate to them, and the remaining 53%, that, as Spurgeon says, 'We will do anything we can to serve them,' and as Jesus says, 'Love your neighbour as yourself.'[4]

The increasing traction of #LoveYourNeighbour on social media, particularly in diverse cities such as Birmingham, shows that many people are keen to strengthen the connection between faith in action and being rooted in their locality. If you look for 'Slow Church' on social media you'll find a celebration of a local focus: 'We need practices that reorient our desire to our places. Reorientation towards place is nothing less than a spiritual discipline.'[5]

In short: bloom where you are planted.

Because a simple invitation can help churches grow

You can invest a huge amount in your building—but unless you communicate, unless you invite people, don't assume they will come. I know that it's not all about bums on seats—and there's more on this in the next section—but the fact is that if the Church in the UK does not grow it will die. In 2016 the Archbishop of Canterbury said that evangelism is not an app, an optional add-on. It's the whole operating system. This is not about territory building, but about recognising the necessity of community for Christian growth.

It's easy to believe the lie that 'no one would want to come to my church', but if they're not invited you'll never know—and perhaps the invitation will at least be the catalyst for their going somewhere else that suits them. 'Back to Church Sunday' encouraged people to issue the invite. In the Diocese of Lichfield alone 6,000 people went to church after being invited. Six months later half of these were still in touch, and around one in eight were regularly attending.[6]

Theologian Lesslie Newbigin described the church as 'the hermeneutic of the gospel… The many activities by which we seek to challenge public life with the gospel—evangelistic campaigns, distribution of Bibles and Christian literature, conferences, and even books… have power to accomplish their purpose only as they are rooted in and lead back to a believing community.'[7] Invitation is at the heart of our faith.

I was struck by the story of a new church staff member who used his first two weeks in the job to visit the homes of all the families who had a loose connection with the church, perhaps through a christening, wedding or toddler group, and invite them in person to a new family afternoon café-style service.[8]

Communication is about relationship, not just as individuals, but as a church with the community. Genuine friends will expect an invite, and certainly won't hate us for offering one. Contacts and acquaintances won't be surprised. With strangers we have nothing to lose and everything to gain.

We need to do our bit—and leave the results to God.

Because a simple message can change perceptions and lives

In England, at least a third of adults have never had any significant connection to any church. Perhaps as many as a quarter have had a connection at some point, but not now. You'll have heard the quote: the church is the only institution that exists for the sake of its non-members. Communication outside our bounds matters because our 'non-members' need the gospel just as much as we do. The gap may be wide, but we need to bridge it.

An increasing number of people have a very limited preconception of church and Christianity. Their position is one of ignorance rather than prejudice. This means we cannot assume they have mental barriers to our message. But nor can we assume that people know who Jesus is, or what the gospel has to offer them.

Everyone at least has the right to hear about Jesus, however they choose to respond! Who are we to deny them that? As Paula Gooder puts it, 'We can immerse ourselves in the most loving of deeds but if, at the end, those whom we have loved know nothing more of Jesus than they did at the beginning, have we not, in some way, failed them?'[9]

What we communicate—intentionally or not—will always be far broader than anything we can control. There is freedom for us in this. The failures and successes of our communication may well be unseen and unknown. But we can make every effort to 'go into all the world and preach the gospel to all creation' (Mark 16:15).

Reasons people don't bother with communications

'No one notices'

It's true that we have the blind spots of the over-familiar, perhaps to a scruffy, unloved noticeboard that's been there forever. Our neighbours may have the same blind spots to it, but it is a total lie that changes wouldn't be noticed. If you updated the magazine or banners they'd read into this a renewed sense of energy and purpose, whether or not they like what you produce. God may look on the heart, but people certainly do still look on the outside.

'Does it need improving?'

'Possibly, but it doesn't really matter that much.' Translation: I can't bear the prospect of the conversations about it, let alone the one with the person who did it so badly last time. The fear of upsetting people in church can come from genuine pastoral care. Other times it's just fear, and we know what the Bible says about that. There are many times when the wellbeing of the person is more important than the task; when the relationship should delay the review. There's discernment needed. But if our vision for what could take place is clear and inspiring enough, you may find support in the most unlikely place.

The Talking Jesus research (2016) suggests that 20% of the population are open to knowing more about being a Christian.

'We've got some stuff to work through first'

This is particularly true of churches in transition, churches in a leadership hiatus, or churches wrestling through the best approach to reaching their neighbourhood. For example, should the church be attractional or missional? Both are words you'll probably hear only in a church context. The ideas are not mutually exclusive, but rather reflect a creative tension between either communicating 'Come to our event' or sending people out in a more organic way, where communication will be more personal than corporate, more informal than formal.

These are great things for any church to work through in 21st-century Britain, but they are not a reason to press pause on outreach, evangelism or external communication. It may be that working out these issues while using the tools in chapter 3 helps clarify your vision, or understand your mission context more clearly.

Sometimes a desire to grow in prayer or work through theological issues means you neglect the simple task of just welcoming people. Revelation: it's okay to welcome people into mess and on to the journey, even if you haven't yet got to the destination. God is good at working through mess.

'Too much time, cost and effort'

Time, money and strength for the effort are resources we all feel we lack, but that God has to give. Complacency in something as important as church communications can accidentally damage the mission of the church, inhibit change and discourage everyone. Colossians 3:23 seems relevant here: 'Whatever you do, work at it with all your heart, as working for the Lord, not for human masters.' If this means drawing on help, such as this book, or training, it's worth it.

Case studies of churches that gave the time, effort and money to launch new initiatives or change their buildings for their community have been compiled by the Churches Trust for Cumbria.[10] One of the most revealing is from a church where it didn't all go to plan, where the 'difficult but brave and honest' decision was made that the project was too large. These are the lessons they learned with the benefit of hindsight, which can help others overcome practical barriers:

- Consider the needs of the community first and the buildings second. 'Co-produce' with community members.
- Create a fun event to give people ideas of what is possible, like a trial run.
- Identify small tasks so that everyone feels that they can contribute without fearing that they are going to be burdened forever.
- Don't rely on just one or two people, as this makes the project vulnerable.[11]

At the other extreme, the example of well-resourced churches can be intimidating. If we are searching for technical perfection with unskilled volunteers or a limited budget, we might lose the creativity of the quick idea. There are opportunities for creative experiments in church communications where the consequences for failure are actually very low… but if they touch a nerve, spark an interest or use a new talent, the potential is enormous. Have a go. It doesn't need to be perfect. It really doesn't.

Sometimes the improvements we'd like to make are prevented by the most boring realities: the building isn't suitable; we couldn't get planning permission; we weren't granted a faculty (which will mean nothing to those outside the Church of England, and far too much possibly to a PCC member); we didn't know where to get funds. Helpful resources are listed in chapter 4, and if our church budget is 'theology in figures', as the Archbishop of Canterbury has described it,[12] remember that sometimes the most boring things are actually integral to our outreach. They're evangelism, not administration. Don't give up before you've even started.

Summary: why it matters

The National Churches Trust has found that 86% of the UK population have been in a church at some point in the last year. This includes 40% of British adults of other religions.[13] Fresh expressions of church are growing. There is so much potential.

And yet many people don't know Jesus even really existed. Our external communication is essential to keep awareness high, in the hope that one day it will translate into action.

Yes, it's easy to feel the accusation of those outside the church: 'You're so behind the times.' We may feel an accusation from this book: 'You should be doing more.' But as I've said in the other books in this series, there's no condemnation here. Those in churches tirelessly serving their communities and God deserve support and respect, not further demands. Churches experience regular moments to choose between complacency and conviction. Complacency is easy. Conviction is exciting. Challenging, but exciting.

When we communicate as a church, in action, in truth, it is an act of love.

2

What to consider first

Before you set out to grapple properly with all the ways you communicate outside the church, there are five strategic questions that can form the foundation of a long-term plan. Ideally take these and discuss them with a group.

1. What is our current reality?
2. What is our core message?
3. Who is our focus?
4. Are we communicating a cohesive, consistent, credible identity?
5. Are our expectations realistic and shared?

Leading Your Church into Growth is a resource that takes the necessary time and space to walk you through these areas and more. The workbook alone, redesigned in 2016, is thought-provoking, well designed and full of nuggets of truth, an excellent resource for any church. For example, the course encourages churches to think through how much they put into prayer, presence, proclamation and persuasion. Research into churches that did this found that average attendance rose by 16%, but 92 churches had made no changes, and their attendance fell nine per cent. Conclusion? 'If churches want to grow they need to change, if they don't change they wither and die'.[14] Find out more at www.leadingyourchurchintogrowth.org.uk.

1. What is our current reality?

First, your current reality is that you are in stiff competition. Not with local churches, and seriously there is no excuse for that; there's no shortage of people for us all to reach, and fighting among ourselves is destructive beyond anything we can imagine. Loving your neighbour needs to begin with us. Unity among churches should be something we always seek to communicate. God honours unity. Jesus prayed for it. Celebrate the successes of others. Support, don't judge. I could continue, but will resist—just read Jesus' prayer in John 17!

We're in competition not with each other, but with everything else around us. Nicola David, in her great Grove booklet on *Publicity and the Local Church*, puts it this way:

What you are in competition for is mindshare. You are up against TV ads, 48-sheet hoardings, magazines, websites, shop windows, video games. They all employ the language of the market—fast-moving, clever, colourful, visual, expensive, challenging, sexy, even—all packed with evangelistic messages for products and services, 'Try me and your life will be better!' This is also what Jesus said, and what we are trying to say on his behalf. And yet our promise is the only one that can be relied upon![15]

No pressure then.

It's true though: Jesus' message stands apart, because we are increasingly savvy to the manipulation of advertising, and amid this noise the bell of truth can chime above the rest.

You can audit your external communications first by going through all the tools listed in chapter 3 and discussing with at least one other person—preferably someone from outside the church as well as someone from inside—how each might be perceived. For example, a glass entrance might be perceived as being open and welcoming. It also might be perceived as being expensive. Of course perceptions are subjective, but this is a useful exercise in removing blind spots.

You may have heard the definition of insanity, commonly attributed to Einstein, as doing something over and over again and expecting a different result. The next questions are 'How long has this been like this? Is it due a makeover? Or are we just being insane, expecting growth without change?'

Assessing current reality might also mean stating as a group any known targets (for example in a Mission Action Plan), any known constraints (funding and planning), and any known risks (internal disagreement, transitions).

Finally, and this is the fun bit, list all the things you have to promote, everything you think you can already offer your community. This will include the message you teach on a Sunday, probably your weekly activities, possibly use of your building for prayer or events, perhaps courses like Alpha, and definitely an opportunity to explore the great questions of Christianity asked in the public space.

2. What is our core message?

When Christian Publishing and Outreach (CPO), where I work, produces new external resources for churches it encourages them to ask this question: Are you trying to welcome? Invite? Bless? Provoke? This might make a big difference to the resources you require.

Welcomes and invitations are aimed at those who might want to come. Ideal for carol services, or perhaps for people with an existing connection.

Seeking to bless might involve a Bible verse or a prayer. It might take the form of little pastoral cards with verses on them, or scripture art.[16] Encouragement is at its heart, something churches at their best do better than anyone else. Our encouragement may be publicising a course for the good of the community—like a marriage course.

Seeking to provoke is very different. It is aimed at the ambivalent, those ignorant of Christianity, or perhaps even those who are antagonistic towards 'religion'. It is not pointing to church. It is pointing to God, or to self-reflection, or to the questions we ask ourselves. It takes a risk. It stimulates discussion. It keeps awareness and interest high. It might be humorous, or topical. National campaigns from Christmas Starts with Christ and Alpha have provided some excellent examples of this over many years. From when I was a kid I remember stark black and white posters for a Billy Graham crusade with anagrams of LIFE and a question ('ILE.F What does it mean?', 'FE.LI What does it mean?). I remember them! Perhaps you remember them. That's the whole point. Create something memorable.

Welcome, invite, bless, provoke… The other message you might be communicating is 'This is who we are', which could relate to any one of those four. This might look like:

- A photo of faces of people in your community.
- Examples of where you're serving the community, perhaps under the banner of 'Love your neighbour' or 'HOPE' or a local campaign such as #londonunited.
- A screen showing video and images of what takes place at the church.

You also might want to communicate who you are in the most literal sense: your name, contact details and core values, mission statement, vision. There is more discussion of this in the other book in this series, *Church from the Inside*, and there are examples of a range of church statements in the toolkit.

3. Who is our focus?

Everyone, you say! We want to reach everyone! Of course. Narrowing it down, however, will help you be effective. Outside the church, who notices you? Those who walk by. Other churches. Groups that use the building. The local school (you hope). Local government or charities. Individuals who read the magazine, or check your website or social media. Does it go wider than this?

This is your network. This is your current reach.

Now ask yourself—how well do you know each of these groups? For a fascinating local insight go to www.datashine.org.uk and zoom into your patch. You can choose the census data criteria you want to display, for example 'Origins and Belief'/Religion/ Those who said they had "no religion"'. The site then colour codes the map accordingly, and will show you the percentage down to street level. I discovered that around two-thirds of people on my street in Brighton said they had no religion, whereas along the coast in Worthing there are areas where two-thirds identify as Christian. In some parts of London and Birmingham two-thirds identify as Muslim. This affects how we communicate. One size does not fit all.

I also discovered that most of my street walk to work, which tells me that they probably notice any major visual changes within a five-minute radius, probably enough to take a close look. If I'm anything to go by, they also like cafes, and there are plenty to choose from.

For a church this is what a marketing person might deem a potential angle, a hook, a clue. Around a third live on their own. There aren't many teenagers. Another insight. One church joined with another congregation ten minutes' drive away, perhaps realising that although the houses there were bigger, education levels were significantly lower. Data like this on this scale is never going to reveal individual needs and preferences, but it will help you think about how your church can both identify community needs, and be relevant in its communication.

Other books in this series talk about 'personas' that marketing organisations use to identify those they are trying to reach. It might be a woman in her sixties with strong community connections and a cultural affiliation with church. It might be a couple in their twenties with no experience of religion. This may be largely determined by your geographical area. If your church is in an affluent village, your communication outside the church may be different in subtle and obvious ways to that of a church in a socially deprived suburb.

The point is this: all strategy needs to begin with WHO. To listen clearly to those outside the church you could:

1. Use datashine and the other tools listed at the back of this book to find data about your neighbours and build a picture of your community.
2. If you're feeling brave, supplement this by using a story in the local newspaper, an online survey or a questionnaire at a local community group to find out what neighbours think of your church and how you can serve them.

The culture of our church can connect or disconnect in subtle ways with the culture of those around us. This in part explains the success of Fresh Expressions churches, which have grown in the face of decline in other areas. Often focused on a homogenous group, they demonstrate a high awareness of cultural needs and norms. A study of over 500 fresh expressions found that nearly half of people attending had not previously attended church.

The visual designs we use can actively put people off. This is why CPO has worked hard to increase the breadth of the designs it offers to churches, because a stock photo and cheesy pun might make one person smile, and another cringe. If the visual quality and designs outside your church or in your invites and magazine are extremely different from anything you'd see anywhere else in your area you might not be 'distinctive'; you might just seem out of touch.

If the posters are silly, they risk communicating that a church knows it is irrelevant. If the posters are overly pious, they risk communicating that a church is there to chastise.

If people speak English as an additional language, consider information in multiple languages. One church I've seen has posters outside with Bible verses only in Arabic. I can guarantee every Arabic speaker who's sat in a car in the traffic jam outside has read them, but I've also been told they don't get as many white British visitors as they'd like. Be that as it may, the posters communicate that churches are not just for English speakers, and that the Bible is relevant in every language. If in doubt, keep it simple. Simple language will reach more people.

A final word: don't use public platforms for private peeves. Church magazines can be prone to this. The Bible's call to 'submit to one another out of love' can sometimes mean reining in your opinions or agenda. If you've been entrusted with a public voice, steward it wisely or don't be surprised when it gets muted. Similarly, an unnecessarily controversial statement or display can have destructive ripples in a community. If you see one, feel free to take it down, and talk to people in person instead.

Does your church have an established relationship with a school? If so, this specific group of families should be part of your intentional focus. Done well, it might involve some of the following: assemblies (a survey by CPO among churches found that half run assemblies in their local schools), opening the church to school visits, offering parenting courses, involvement in RE lessons or 'collective worship', sending in volunteers to tell Bible stories trained by the excellent Bible Society 'Open the Book' programme, or prayer spaces in schools, an initiative of 24-7 Prayer and a wonderfully creative way for churches to communicate not just with students, but also with their teachers and families. There are more resources relating to all these options in chapter 4.

The focus of your external communication, the 'who', will become clear as you pray for your neighbours and learn to love them. As Pastor Agu Irukwu puts it, 'Our faith and mission will only become authentic at the junction where our love for God is expressed in our love to our neighbours, without compromising the commission to proclaim the gospel unashamedly.'[17]

4. Are we communicating a cohesive, consistent, credible identity?

With this question, you are asking, 'Does our communication match? With itself? With us?' What do people want a church to communicate? Authenticity. What do we want to communicate? Christ—and the good news is that he is always authentic. If we're true to him, and as true as we can be to who we are, then we stand a greater chance of communicating a cohesive, consistent and therefore credible identity.

Very practically, the design style of your external visual communication should ideally match the style inside, and anything you give out too, as well as what people find when they search for your website. If the invitation through the door matches the cover of the magazine, which matches the banner on the building and the poster in the community centre, which matches the image at the front of the website, then people will join the dots and remember you. By means of a branding campaign you will have created a subliminal identity and some awareness, which may be the first step towards interest, desire and action.

5. Are our expectations realistic and shared?

It's not enough to paint a vision of how wonderful things could be. Motivation to change also requires dissatisfaction with the present. You'll need at least one meeting which brings together decision-makers in church leadership with those involved in all aspects of church communication: external, internal, print, digital. Use the questions in this book to identify priorities, then be honest together about your expectations on aims, costs and timescales. If this group can share a vision for what needs to be achieved it will be far easier to convince any doubters in the congregation.

Everyone will benefit from a regular conversation to plan and ensure everything matches as much as possible. One person passionate about banning typos and grammatical errors might be willing to do this for every communication type. Another person with a real eye for graphic design can ensure standards are high across the board.

If you don't have a logo, or want to update your logo, you'll probably need a budget, a designer, and as clear as possible an idea of any colours, images or words you definitely do or don't want. There are organisations who specialise in this listed in chapter 4. A good church logo is simple (not too many colours), works at different sizes, is flexible enough to work against different colour backgrounds, and has an appropriate font for the style of the community.

You might need to standardise the words you use to refer to the church, the church network, your mission statement or your values.

There are rules around photos that I'd hope would be obvious: don't stretch them out of proportion, do make sure they're high enough resolution, don't take them off the internet without permission, do credit any photographers in the church, don't use photos of kids, do use photos that tell a story, not just gurning poses or atmospheric waterfalls.

Companies with any investment in external communications (marketing, advertising or PR) can be obsessed with how to measure ROI (return on investment). Some will measure in percentage growth, or budget targets reached, 'hits' to a website, visitors to an event, subscribers to a publication. Data is useful, and positive measurements may help churches in making a case for funding, or justifying future investment. They will never be the full picture because spiritual impact is notoriously impossible to measure. If you measure the impact of communication outside the church primarily by those coming in, then you have missed its full purpose. Invest in it as mission, as outreach, as evangelism.

3

Essential next steps

Other books in this series suggest the following steps: choose your tool, choose your look, plan your year, plan your contents, find your team. For external communication it is impossible to separate the look and the contents from the tool. So the following pages focus on nine external communication tools:

1. Using the church building
2. Noticeboards
3. Invitations and cards
4. Community magazines
5. Books and tracts
6. Community action and events
7. Billboards, buses and street signs
8. Media and PR
9. Websites and social media

In addition to these, of course, are all the things the individuals in the church are involved in, every workplace, group and friendship. There's not space to explore these here, but how individuals relate in these contexts may communicate more about God and church than any corporate effort.

You might find it helpful to go through the list in the following pages as a small team with these questions in mind:

1. Is this something we could do together with other churches, either locally or nationally? For example, are there national campaigns we could use on our noticeboards, online and in local media?
2. How much can we plan in advance, so that one thing leads naturally on to the next?

It's safe to allow six weeks for communication to filter to everyone and dates to get in the diaries. Plan event communications by counting back further than you'd think. Think 'cross-stream' and 'multiplatform', as the corporate world would put it. You're effectively running a mini campaign, so cover all the bases: posters, banners, invites, flyers, decorating the building, website, social media, plugs from the front, email, text, stories, and of course creative flourishes, which may take up most energy, but could have the most impact.

1. Using the church building

Does the style of your building communicate well about those inside or what you're trying to do? Probably not. A quick look at case studies from church architects shows the breadth of possibilities for change.[18] Those who are serious about helping the fabric of their building reflect and enhance the mission of the church may find the sources of advice listed in chapter 4 helpful, plus guidance on community projects, and books that delve further into this subject.[19]

If you do works on your building you don't want people to think it's being knocked down if you're actually building it up. Use display boards, or possibly large pull-up banners, to show not just what you're doing (perhaps including architecture drawings), but also why you're doing it, your vision, your mission, and how people can support it or get involved. Not too many words. Simple line illustrations may be better.

If you're not changing your building structurally, how can it still look different? Could your doors be open more? A fortress is ironically more inviting to vandals and thieves. Some set times with volunteers and a cuppa may draw in the curious or those wanting prayer—wonderful—but even if no one comes in, they communicate 'open for business'.

'Open for prayer' in large letters can have huge impact, perhaps on an A-board on a street corner, or a simple banner on railings. One school I know have a chalk A-board. Every day they put a Bible verse or motto on one side, and a joke on the other. It always gets read.

I grew up in a maze of tightly packed terraced houses, normal for the suburbs, overwhelming for rural visitors before the days of satnav. On one corner amid the domestic sprawl was a large Gothic church, separated off by a hedge, rather like a mansion protecting itself from the surrounding proles. The hedge was large. You couldn't see over it, you couldn't see under it, and if you had to go through it, you'd be faced by a big closed wooden door on the other side. Hedges and fences are perfectly normal, you might think. Yes, if you're trying to protect something, perhaps hide the contents of your living room from burglars or dissuade intruders. Understandable if you really don't like your neighbours. Thankfully a new vicar arrived, and it seems he did like his neighbours, because the first thing he did was cut the hedge down. All of it. The church seemed exposed without it, naked even. It rose out of the narrow streets like a friendly resident giant, quietly inviting children to veer off the pavement on to the grass and touch its old walls. The church grew beyond expectations and was the crucible for a number of national initiatives. Do you need to cut down some kind of hedge?

Banners on buildings are the next stage. They don't need to be there forever, but are so incredibly effective. Bright colours, not many words, and sometimes enormous sizes. The banners printed by CPO either have eyelets or clips with bungees, or come in freestanding boards, so there are multiple options for display. Neil Pugmire, author of *100 Ways to Get Your Church Noticed*, says this: 'It is possible, of course, to create a banner yourself. Try to resist this temptation as, unless your congregation includes artists and graphic designers, it may look amateur. As this is such a high-profile method of publicity, it's important that it looks as good as possible.'[20]

Meeting in a school or community centre? You may want to use feather flags (sometimes called exhibition flags or banner flags), but quality can vary.

Water-based stands can be useful, or roll-up banners (sometimes called pull-up banners), or a table full of refreshments and snacks…

Other options you may have considered, to communicate that your building is full of life:

- Balloons and streamers.
- Bunting, particularly in summer, perhaps with chairs and tables outside.
- Fairy lights around doors, or spotlights with different colours at entranceways. Freestanding external spotlights can be a good investment, even if only for special events. Proper, tasteful exterior lighting can transform any building.
- The grounds of the building, the lawn, grass, flowers, may be helped by a different approach, such as grasses rather than flowers that tend to die quickly, or even a showcase for sculpture and art. There are arts organisations keen to find churches willing to showcase their commissions.[21]
- Is a projection on to the building a possibility? In Brighton, St Peter's Church in the centre of town projected an enormous question mark on to the spire to advertise an Alpha course. It looked amazing.

Those with limited mobility will notice immediately whether the building communicates that they are welcome. Places of worship as public buildings are legally required to be accessible to all those with physical disabilities—but this is not why we do it. We do it because we don't want anyone to feel that they are excluded from entering a place where they might expect to meet with God.

A ramp for wheelchair access is obvious. Some other areas to consider are reserving parking spaces close to the entrance, widening doors, and using clear contrast and large print on signage. Handrails, clear pathways, stating the presence of induction loops: all these help reduce barriers.

There is guidance on this from Church Care and others,[22] including a template audit from the Diocese of London, who write:

It is important to consider your building in relation to all disabilities, not just those represented in your current congregation. Ultimately the important thing about making your church accessible to people with disabilities is not doing something simply because the law requires it but having an active desire to be inclusive.[23]

2. Noticeboards

When I have delivered training on noticeboards, and when others I've spoken to have done the same, a good result is reconsideration of one very simple question: is your noticeboard actually noticed? If someone is walking by, can they read it? Does it face the right direction, at the right angle? Is it in the place no one goes, or perhaps would a board be more effective in the car park where everyone goes? Is it covered by foliage or a fence? Are the words so tiny you'd need binoculars? If it's near traffic, can you get the gist at 20 mph? Can you see it from across the road or is it just in the wrong place? Do you need more than one, visually consistent with each other, in strategic positions?

Start with this: is it visible?

Next, before anyone reads the words, *what does its condition say about your condition*? Revd Adrian Smith (Diocese of Lincoln) has previously encouraged people to learn lessons from the boards outside pubs ('Children, dogs and walkers welcome' in bright, handwritten colours), and also from noticeboards so decrepit that the phone number has chipped away. In Enfield Deanery in London, in August 2013, Phillip

Dawson went round and took photos of every single noticeboard and posted them on Pinterest.[24] I had the pleasure of meeting Phillip a few years later, and his enthusiasm for church communication is contagious. The boards in the photos range from the 'most unloved' to the eminently 'cool'. A bad noticeboard isn't neutral. It's detrimental to everything else that you do. Even if it's become invisible to you, it may be the most visible thing about the church to your community. It matters!

If it's time to replace your noticeboards—and do not underestimate the positive impact of the investment—then CPO and others can help. You'll need to allow a minimum of around £500 for a freestanding board, and will need to speak to your denomination about guidelines and permission. The toolkit in chapter 4 and at www.cpo.org.uk/toolkit has links to help you with this There are decisions to make, such as position, size, wall/post/rail mounted, square or rounded edges, large or small changeable areas for posters, and whether these are magnetic, cloth or lockable. Note—these are decisions just to make, not decisions to discuss for six months. The colour should match other signage and internal communication, and not clash with your building or hurt people's eyes. One word of caution from experience: when you're deciding on the quantity and size of changeable areas for posters it's better to have one you can regularly update than lots that get neglected.

Finally—perhaps most importantly—are the words helpful and welcoming? This is not the place to say all you want to say, so choose carefully.

Basic essentials for fixed text on a church noticeboard are:

- church name, website, phone number, email address
- logo if you have one, and your denomination's logo/region if it's relevant or required
- times of your regular meetings, using terms that are understandable, or simple explanation if they're not (if you're not sure, ask a random passerby what 'sung Eucharist' means)

Then consider:

- a statement of welcome (some examples of words from other churches are in the toolkit)
- a concise summary of your vision
- a contact name
- office opening hours (though your website address may make this unnecessary)

Some noticeboards seem to have been used as an opportunity to state an identity ('We are a Fairtrade/inclusive/child-friendly/disability-friendly/traditional/scripture-upholding church'). While these things may be true and laudable, they can risk communicating the agenda of whoever put the board together rather than the full holistic purposes of the church. In terms of a 'hierarchy of information', as website designers would term it, is the top of the list the loudest?

By the way, the flexible space, a frame, is for events, for designs, not for a warning sticker about theft.

Some churches put a Perspex holder for leaflets or booklets on the board or next to it. One lady put some little 'trypraying' booklets in one: 'Week by week people have been taking them. I have kept adding more booklets, a few at a time. The church has prayed specifically for the people who have taken the booklets. That's 50 as of today. I need more booklets!'

This can be a great thing to do, but beware the experience of another church with no fewer than five perspex holders for leaflets on the board, who discovered people removing leaflets not to read them, but to bin them intentionally to prevent others reading them. Better to have one holder and use it well than a row of empty or damaged ones. The community don't care as much about the presentation of your materials as you might wish.

The other vandalism-proof option for noticeboards is digital signage held within the building, but visible from the street through glass, inside and outward-facing. This can be as simple as a screen connected to a PowerPoint presentation. There are providers listed in chapter 4.

Whatever you do, don't do this:

3. Invitations and cards

Sometimes it's what the commercial world call 'direct mail' and you call 'junk mail': the leaflets that come through the door, sometimes in an envelope. Statistics show that, given the choice between taking in information on email or something printed, half of us prefer print, and only one in five prefer email. 82% of direct mail is opened—which is why, even in a digital age, UK charities still spend two-thirds of their advertising budgets on direct mail.[25]

In terms of awareness churches cannot afford not to do this. But don't necessarily expect the 82% who read it to act. Charities spend money knowing full well that only 1.1–1.4% of people will actually respond. So, if you give out 1,000 Christmas invitations, you're doing well if 14 people turn up. If you don't, maybe no one will.

How do we up the odds? Packaging your invitation in a Christmas card may help. The Royal Mail in 2016 found that 72% would prefer a card to say 'Happy Christmas'. It's more likely to sit on someone's mantelpiece, especially if it looks good. If it matches the church's Christmas publicity online and in noticeboards and adverts, even better. One church in Bicester who use a school building rather than a church dropped a Christmas and Easter card into 1,000 homes. With local images and a nativity scene, the Christmas message inside talked about the connection of Jesus' birth to the local community. It also—and this is clever—had a photo of the summer fun day from six months earlier, because without the visual reference of a church building it joined the dots between a very public activity and a more hidden Sunday community.

Even if people don't respond by coming to a service, they may respond privately to the message about Christmas inside the card. This is why CPO always provides template designs, print, and an optional form of words explaining the meaning of Christmas and Easter, so that invitations as cards or leaflets say much more than just 'Come to us'. They also say, 'God has come to you'.

In Petersfield the churches join together every year to door-drop all the neighbours, with a design produced by the local school. With details of all celebrations at all churches, it communicates unity as well as information.

It doesn't cost much. To give you an idea, in 2017 1,000 invites, depending on format, could cost less than £100. Split between a few churches this is a small cost. Options on print formats are:

- Paper 'tri-folds' (also known as 'brochures' on some software such as Publisher, or as a 'DL', a printing term) are great for groups of churches with loads of information.
- Paper A5 flyers are popular because they're cheap but are also more disposable. It usually doesn't cost much more to print on both sides, and if you have only one side's worth of information, duplicate it so it shows however it falls.
- Postcards, flat A6 size, lend themselves to a strong image on one side, and plenty of detail on the back. They are cheaper than you'd assume, and are more likely to get propped up and stick around.
- Folded cards may get put on a shelf, and give the option for an image and words either on one side or up to three. CPO are one of many companies who could print your words inside and your logo on the back.
- Business cards are also an option, especially with a strong image and very few words (for example, 'Free lunch club every Tuesday', or 'Your local church: St Matthew's, 10.30 every Sunday. All welcome').

As well as including the basic what/who/when/where/why, think into the situation of those coming: do you need to include information about childcare, parking, refreshments, public transport? Is it an opportunity to talk about other, related activities that happen more regularly, or to mention your website and social media?

Churches adept at door-dropping allocate streets to volunteers, and encourage them to pray as they walk and drop. It can be a great way for everyone to get involved. The Neighbourhood Prayer Network, Adopt-A-Street, and the National Prayer Weekend can help with combining prayer and invitation. On Rogation Sunday many Anglican churches prayer walk around the parish boundary. 'Beating the bounds', as it used to be called, is all about 'claiming the ground', praying for your neighbours alone or in a group.

While this method is good for 'comprehensive coverage', especially in isolated settings, it doesn't work in every context (where I live the number of flats makes it virtually impossible), and it will always be trumped by something given from hand to hand, person to person, situation to situation, face to face. This is where you really reach beyond the

1.4%, but more importantly, may get to talk about the invitation too. The first people to give it to are probably those who connect with your building during the week: the parents from the toddler group and the visitors.

You don't need to use an invitation. Try news, updates, 'this is who we are', which can take the form of a small leaflet, or could be more regular, such as a community magazine.

4. Community magazines

'Parish Pump' was set up in 1999 to be a well of content initially for a very small number of magazines. It now resources thousands of them. Why? As founder Anne Coomes writes, 'church magazine editors help the people in their church to stay in touch with each other, but they can do even more. They can help their church to stay in touch with its community. A church magazine can bravely go through letterboxes into homes where no minister has gone before! In fact, your church magazine may be the only Christian contact that many people in your community will ever have.'[26] What an enormous opportunity.

In a 2016 CPO survey of UK church magazine editors, the vast majority expected their magazine to be read by neighbours who don't attend church (84%), and also by local businesses (48%) and local government (31%). One magazine has the Prime Minister as a reader! Another sends a copy to the local newspaper and radio. Despite this enormous influence, two thirds struggle for regular contributors, and a third struggle for distributors. If you are not personally involved in your church magazine, how can you support it better?

If you are involved, you are probably trying to provide:

- a regular expression of your church's Christian presence and witness to the neighbourhood
- a reflection of the social life of the local Christian community (your church!)
- a statement of Christian beliefs on various issues
- a schedule of events at your church (plus the times and venues)

Make the magazine available on your website if you can, and ensure it has as many visual links as possible to the rest of your church communications, whether through a logo, the same font as the newssheet, or the same design on the front cover as on the posters. So many church magazines are cramped with multiple fonts and dodgy clipart. Two fonts are better, with plenty of space to aid readability. There are suggestions on free images at the back of this book. Avoid jargon and 'in' language. Show that the church is part of the local community, not set apart. There are resources in the toolkit to assist church magazine editors with the practicalities.

Take time once in a while to look at the subtext rather than the text. In other words, forget the grammar for a moment and ask what is communicated overall. Is the subtext actually quite negative? Are you accidentally communicating that you are a clique of people who all look the same, that religion is full of rituals, that people outside the church are judged and patronised, or a target for conversion? Does it look like Christians think they have all the answers, when those reading probably have doubts?

Conversely, a magazine is a chance to communicate that:

- The church is active in helping the poor.
- Christians are aware of needs around the world.
- Prayer seems to have an impact on people's lives.
- People in church are welcoming of everyone.
- God is relevant to people today in the place where I live.
- The Bible says some interesting stuff.
- People in church have a sense of humour.
- People in church clearly care.

This is a story worth telling, and a message worth the effort of compiling, designing and printing a magazine.

5. Books and tracts

When the Queen turned 90 in 2016 a group of charities put together a book about her faith, *The Servant Queen*, designed to be high-quality enough to treasure as a gift, and affordable enough for churches to buy in bulk to give out in person. They did. CPO shipped a million copies in just six months. There are many reasons it was so successful, but one is that people were proud to give it, and genuinely grateful not just to receive it, but to keep it and read it. It was given in the context of relationship and generosity.

Undoubtedly God can use tracts and outreach booklets handed to strangers on the street. In some parts of London, at least at a certain time of day, you're guaranteed to receive one, and possibly an offer of prayer too. This can literally work wonders. However, a high-quality, professionally designed and written gospel 'giveaway', when it's combined with friendship and the right moment (it needs to be the right moment), can be a more effective means of communication. UK publishers have worked hard at producing fresh resources you'd feel comfortable giving to a friend. There are also some excellent apologetics books written for different audiences, and you'll know, if you read them, whether they're right for your friend.

I remember Cathy on my table at an Alpha course suddenly remembering a booklet she'd been given years ago by someone she'd liked and respected, in fact the only Christian she'd ever met. 'I've never read it, of course, but for some reason I've never thrown it away either… I'll read it tonight.' That night it changed her life.

6. Community action and events

With all this focus on the printed word, it's good to remember 1 John 3:18: 'Let us not love with words or speech but with actions and in truth'! When the church engages locally in action, it communicates more powerfully than by any words. The preceding two verses talk about laying down our lives, and noticing material needs.

Your church is probably already involved in social action in some way. Chapter 4 has links to organisations that can resource, support, equip and inspire you in your particular area. Here is one example of the many hundreds that might inspire you in your context: New Life Baptist Church near Nottingham, with help from the Cinnamon Trust, used the five 'paths to wellbeing' identified by the New Economics Foundation (connect, give, be active, keep learning, take notice) to establish a 'community centre to promote wellbeing', with a cafe. The language connects. The need is real. The content is unashamedly Christian, with daily prayer and meditation 'for anyone wanting to seek peace and meet with God', led by pastor Ruth Rice, who describes herself on the website (accurately, from my knowledge of her!), as 'passionate about helping people connect with God and each other and helping all ages find balance in their lives'.[27] The model is now being replicated in many other places.

This is an example of a regular community presence. Food banks, debt relief centres (often connected to the excellent Christians Against Poverty) and night shelters are others. I've known many people outside church form a relationship with a church by volunteering for these activities. As soon as you show up to help, as soon as people see churches living out their faith in this way, and especially if you do it with other churches, the communication 'points' outweigh many sermons.

The theological imperative to live public lives of justice is outlined with great depth and practicality in Ruth Valerio's 2016 book *Just Living*. If you need to work with your local council, Roger Sutton, a champion for church engagement in community need, has helpfully put together 20 golden nuggets, free to download.[28] For example: be united, go to the top and work down, ask what they need and learn the lingo!

Some churches use outdoor services. This may actually be the time to unlearn the lingo, or at least replace some of it in public. Impenetrable ritual, anything too wordy or too long won't communicate well. Activities with interaction and creativity, perhaps drama, face-paints, balloons, dance, songs that people can join in, will probably work better.

If you can't imagine a church service in your context, how about something less traditional? Beyond Church in Brighton open beach huts as an Advent calendar. Another church offers 'readings' and prayer in places very accustomed to tarot cards. There are 'healing rooms' in churches across the country, where people drop in and have a spiritual experience they never expected. Lumina is one organisation that goes to mind, body and spirit fairs, knowing that many people are hungry for an experience of God, and need someone to show them how to find it.

The Healing on the Streets ministry sends people out to pray for shoppers and passers-by. The Brighton group describe the five 'marks' of what they do—that is, what they're trying to communicate—as the presence of the Holy Spirit, peace, gentleness, love and compassion.[29] It has some similarities to Treasure Hunting, a form of prophetic evangelism on the streets that came out of Bethel Church in the US. Sussex priest Jules Middleton in her award-winning blog Picking Apples of Gold describes it like this: 'Basically it means praying and asking God for some clues as to the people he wants you to reach out to in your town/venue/area. Then you go out looking for what God has shown you.' Jules has put together some really helpful guidelines to use if this is something your church would like to try in the community.[30]

Think about a rhythm of mission and special events through the year. Here are some examples CPO has been involved in, and HOPE also has stacks of ideas, case studies and resources.[31]

Easter

Taking the biblical Stations of the Cross, the One Friday initiative encourages churches to retell the passion of Jesus through art trails and drama. One village put Jenny Hawke's art as laminated posters in unexpected places such as a shop and a bus stop, and gave free copies of a booklet with Bible passages at each location. Another gave the scripture passages to small groups with a piece of garden trellis and asked them to express the theme artistically; all the designs were combined in an exhibition. In Manchester a high school displayed Micah Purnell's posters in the entrance hall as conversation starters, and in South Shields a church rented a shop for hospitality and prayer during Lent, with art as the backdrop.

Passion plays in outside areas never fail to draw onlookers. The Passion Trust has been set up to support these. Why? Because, as their website reminds people, in a 2014 Bible Society survey, 43% of children had never read about or heard of the crucifixion, or seen it portrayed.[32]

Summer

Churches are experts at fun days. The charity Fusion Youth and Community are among those that provide advice. One church that ran a community festival on the Isle of Dogs said, 'Our first festival was a huge step of faith for us, as a small church… But with 2,000 people coming along, and five churches joining us… [it's] been hugely helpful in raising the profile of local churches and bringing us all together under one banner, and I would wholeheartedly recommend them to anyone who wants to make a difference in their community.' Another describes their 'open crowd' festival as 'the best missional activity we have done in our church over the last two years', and yet another says running a festival 'marked a breaking through into being more a part of our community…

[It] gave us a vision for more. God has amazed us in the doors he has opened.'[33] The fun day may be as simple as a barbecue, bouncy castle and loads of games, but it's an excuse to build relationships and create community.

Christmas

'Beer and carols' at Christmas in local pubs has grown in popularity. From 2014 to 2016 a group of charities (Tearfund, HOPE, Sports Chaplaincy UK and Integrity Music) joined together to produce a carol sheet explaining the meaning behind the words, designed as something people would want to keep and read. It enabled carol services to take place in sports clubs, stadiums, clubs and community centres.

I went carol singing from lamppost to lamppost in central Brighton with a group of friends from church. It surprised me how deviant it felt, how subversive, to be singing out those words outside blocks of flats, bars and cafes. One lady hung out of the window to listen, then came down to thank us, saying it was the highlight of her Christmas. Carol singing every year will mean that people look forward to seeing you!

Messy Nativity is a great idea: knitted sheep in a trail, culminating in an open-air nativity. The Big Picture creates a nativity scene in the community. Social media is useful for finding other ideas and campaigns. 'Christmas Starts with Christ' encourages churches to start the conversation, with a simple, free, universal logo to use in public places.

Christmas is the one time of year when community activity around you of some kind is guaranteed. People really will expect the church to play a part. They will expect signs of festivity outside the church building and warmth inside.

Your community activity or event can be as simple as mince pies, candles and a drink offered to passers-by, hopefully with an invitation to a carol service, and some festive clothes and music for good measure. Decorations and presents always top the lists of things that make Brits feel festive, so could you host a Christmas market or a craft afternoon to make decorations? They are a way in to pointing to the source of the celebration. Finally, look at what Jesus taught and modelled on community celebration. This year could you host a meal for those who are homeless, seeking asylum, friendless or isolated?

7. Billboards, buses and street signs

Did you know that of all the forms of advertising, outdoor advertising is projected to grow faster than any other except mobile over the next five years? And that the biggest mobile brand in the world, Apple, is the biggest single advertiser for Clear Channel, the UK's biggest billboard company? As its chief executive says, 'What you want for your brand is fame. If you want fame, you need mass reach. Outdoor advertising is still the best way of getting that message across. We talk about the power of the public promise. If a brand is confident enough to put itself out there, that sends a powerful message about the brand itself. People like to buy brands other people know about. It is about public accountability. You can't ad-block a billboard; it is there on the street'.[34]

Christianity has lacked presence in OOH (Out-of-Home) advertising, as it's called, perhaps owing to a lack of confidence or the right type of message. There are exceptions. ChurchAds have had huge impact over the years with 'pre-evangelistic' campaigns such as 'Christmas Starts with Christ'. Alpha's campaigns have been all over buses across the country. Particularly in Scotland, the trypraying campaign (www.trypraying.org.uk) has been active in securing adverts on buses and bus shelters simply saying 'trypraying'. This was Sharon in Edinburgh's response: 'I saw the advert on the buses on Southbridge and it was such a clear and simple message that both my friend and I have actually started to pray... It has had a big impact on me. Thank you for reminding us all about God in this very materialistic world.'[35]

Trypraying is about initiating conversations about God, with the help of a little trypraying booklet. It encourage churches to work with other churches in their area. David Hill, the founder, says, 'It makes a great impact and demonstrates a unity in the gospel. It also opens up more possibilities of putting things into the public space with advertising. A minister from a church in a town where trypraying was being used went on a school visit recently—all of the kids knew where the trypraying banners were in the town, and a number were happy to receive the kids' booklet. In all places there is hunger for spiritual reality, and in all places it is okay to have conversations about our faith.' If you want to put up bus signs you can find advice in chapter 4.

Even without a campaign, does your church have a simple street sign? Church communications trainer Neil Pugmire reminds us that 'all your careful effort to communicate activities will be no use if no one can actually find your church. Even if someone never passes your building, if they pass a road sign featuring your church's name they may subconsciously take in where to find it.'[36] You may need to apply to the local authority highway department in writing.

8. Media and PR

Why do we engage with the media? Because it reaches thousands, and the potential benefits are greater than the risks. Christians need to work at maintaining a strong voice in the media, and be intentional about amplifying that voice. In 2016 I was asked to interview senior clergy and lay church members in the Diocese of London on their use of digital communications. One of the questions was around what they felt the church ought to be communicating publicly. Answers were united: 'It's about getting people to realise the church is there, and what we're doing is good. We need good news; personal stories; people, parishes, projects, grassroots. We need to reach those not in the church by showing how the church is serving the city.'

There is an immense opportunity here, and it can start at a simple level. First, take a morning to make sure every single 'what's on in my town' website, paper and magazine has details of all your regular activities, with links to your website and contact details. If you're giving the information over email rather than a contact form, use it as an opportunity to introduce yourself as a point of contact 'if they'd ever like any more information or stories about the church's activities/events in the community'. If you have a major event you may be able to use your poster design for a simple press advert, budget allowing.

Local newspapers, magazines, websites and blogs are desperate for 'human interest stories', and churches are full of them. If they don't come looking, go to them with the kind of thing you can imagine being of interest. For example:

- A special event for the whole community, ideally in the future or possibly very recent.
- A celebration of volunteering, either locally or overseas, with personal stories.
- An anniversary, of people in the church or the church itself.
- A story of faith, of life transformation, of healing.
- An activity which relates to national issues (for example, a food bank while poverty is in the news). If it's unusual, or new, even better.

Relationship helps, but it doesn't need to be the sole responsibility of the church leader. The key publicity person could be anyone. You'll need email addresses for current contacts, but meet people in person if you can, so that you're giving them what is needed. With emails, keep them brief, include links, and don't bother with attachments unless they're high resolution images (probably a PDF).

Do: mentally plan your main points for any phone calls, make the communication simple and short (200 words maximum), stick to the facts. You'll need a simple subject, a summary paragraph saying who/what/when/where/how, some quotes, a sense of the wider context, and finally, some very clear contact details.

Don't: pester, send something at an irrelevant date, or out of work hours; forget to proofread (journalists will notice).

There is excellent advice on media liaison and radio phone-ins in Neil Pugmire's book and website *100 Ways to Get Your Church Noticed*. He also talks about crisis PR. PR is public relations—so to an extent everything in this chapter is about PR. (One church described their massive banner for 'healing and prayer here' on a road full of traffic jams as 'great PR'.) Public relations are harder when the news is bad. In a crisis situation where the church has found itself at the centre of bad news, there are ways to respond to the media that present the church in a better light than the fearful (and negative) 'no comment'. There are questions to ask about how much any reporter actually knows, whether it is accurate, and whether there is time to call back with a considered response (even if this is just an explanation of why a comment isn't possible yet). This process can be repeated, and there may be time after the dust has settled to go back to the same person with a positive message or story about the outcome or changes that have been made.

Experienced church communications officer Anna Drew advises preparing well in advance: 'What really is the worst that could happen?' She also reminded me of the scene in the TV series *Blackadder* where the 'fool' Baldrick writes his name on a bullet and keeps it hidden, so that the 'bullet with his name on it' can't hit him. Figure out what your bullet is. What's the absolute hardest question you could be asked, say, on live radio? If you've prepared, if it's got your name on it but it's in your hands, it can't kill you. It is worth noting that all church denominations run joint training through www.churchcommstraining. org, and professional assistance in a crisis may well be available through your denomination.

9. Websites and social media

If your church doesn't have a website, or if you all agree that your website is rubbish, this needs to be top of the list for communicating outside the church. There are plenty of places to start at www.cpo.org.uk/toolkit, and step-by-step advice in the *Church Online* books in this series.

Why? Because anyone visiting your church is likely to check the website first. Because anyone using your building will expect relevant information to be online. Because it is the most cost-effective, far-reaching and relevant way to have a presence in your neighbours' homes, on their phones, in their pocket. There is no longer any excuse for churches not to have a presence online, at the very least on directories such as www.findachurch.co.uk and www.achurchnearyou.com.

Your website and social media should complement and enhance your other external communications. For example:

- Comment on any events or news stories that are being publicised.
- Put up pictures of current or forthcoming events.

- If you use a picture of your church building or the noticeboard, find images of people to go with it.
- Use logo, colours and fonts that are consistent with everything printed.
- On social media, intentionally follow and engage with other local organisations and groups.

One church was setting up a new service in a new part of town. They set up a community Facebook group, and within a couple of weeks had hundreds of people connected. Before the doors had even opened there was a tangible momentum, connection and community.

Another church, Christ Church Southgate (@ChristChurchN14) decided to externalise their internal communication by putting regular pictures on Facebook, by posting photos of flyers and posters, and also by creating a little 'GIF' of photos (using the free tool www.gifmaker.me), so that those scrolling through on social media could see an instant slideshow. One local person said, 'I love being a "follower" of this lively joy-filled church! Inspiring.'

Find your team

A communications team with a mix of skills and personalities, probably all volunteers, all committed (we hope) to the same central aim, can achieve the same level of fundamental improvement as a full-time staff member. I've seen it happen.

Potential new recruits might be:

- Those most involved in the local community, able to see what you do from the perspective of their neighbours.
- One of their friends, for an outside view.
- Those passionate about contextual mission.
- Exhibition-goers, photographers, people with graphic design on their walls at home, and opinions about fonts.
- Those who can offer constructive feedback on the magazine, or suggestions on Christmas/Easter publicity.
- Anyone who's taken the initiative to improve communication for their ministry, small group or club.
- A church leader committed to growing the church.

When working with a communications team these four principles can be helpful:

1. Share a foundation of grace and truth. I love the description of Jesus in John 1:14 as 'the one and only Son, who came from the Father, full of grace and truth'. It can mean replacing the hard lines with soft. It can require us to say the difficult thing in love, forgive each other's failings, but maintain high expectations.

2. Know who is responsible for what. Job descriptions may be going a step too far, but there's something to be said for clarifying expectations clearly and regularly, so that the person doing one thing doesn't get blamed for something entirely out of their remit or role.

3. Aim for minimal 'drama'. Internal communication can be prime storm-in-a-teacup territory for churches, up there with the song choice and the youth night. If you find yourselves in a heated discussion over a poster or misplaced parenthesis it's time for a perspective check.

4. Know when criticism is constructive and when it's just criticism. Can we fix it, even just for next time? There is no excuse for actively discouraging others in a church in the name of 'just being honest', particularly on something as important as communication.

This is the only method I've used to mobilise volunteers. First, pray. Next, think whom you would most want to respond if you did a big callout to the whole congregation. Then, pray for the right opportunity to ask that person outright in a way that gives them the chance to think and pray about it themselves.

Volunteer mobilisation and evangelism have this in common: there's nothing, no other form of communication on earth, more powerful than one person speaking honestly to another, powered by prayer.

One final word. The very best teams won't be confined to church members. They may include:

- Non-Christian neighbours.
- People in other local churches. I love the vision of the Creative Missions teams in the US who send communications taskforces to small churches in need of help. Perhaps there is a local church with different resources you could work with. If another church has a great design person, would they be willing to spend an hour or two with you? If you have an experienced editor, could they give constructive help to someone down the road?
- Worldwide support. There is a list in the toolkit

of great blogs where you can subscribe to email support, including ideas from CPO. Magazine editors can get help from Parish Pump and the Association of Church Magazine Editors.

- Training providers. Neil Pugmire, author of *100 Ways to Get Your Church Noticed*, and Joe Gallant, from the Church Train blog, are two people (among others) who could travel to your area to share their expertise and give support in church communications. Also look out for conferences and one-off sessions from the denominations and the Evangelical Alliance among others.

Summary

None of this will actually happen without someone to drive it. Once a huge amount of progress has been made in a short time it might plateau for a while, until the next person comes along with energy and motivation to see improvements and make them happen.

If it doesn't feel urgent, if you're concerned it'll never rise to the top of the list, you might need to create a deadline, or a target, or a motivation. You might need to make it SMART (specific, measurable, achievable, realistic, time-bound). I have been known to talk up a crisis to get something changed: 'We really need it by the time *this* happens, because otherwise…' Create an audience: we want to show it off to these people, so let's get it done in time.

One step of improvement might precipitate the next. The risk of failure is pretty low, and the potential is enormous.

What will you do first?

4

Toolkit

Website providers

- www.church123.com
- www.churchedit.com
- www.churchesaliveonline.com
- www.churchinsight.com
- www.ichurch.urc.org.uk
- www.samevine.co.uk
- www.ukchurches.co.uk

Many of these also offer advice and blogs.

For example, for advice on church websites and evangelism, see www.church123.com/design.

There is lots more advice on websites and social media in the other books in this series, or from www.cpo.org.uk/toolkit, where you'll find all these links.

UK church directories

- www.achurchnearyou.com (Church of England only)
- www.findachurch.co.uk (listing over 45,000 UK churches)
- www.searchchurch.co.uk (listing churches that are visitor focused)

Planning permission on adverts and signs

Rules will vary according to area, but as of 2016 temporary event notices up to 0.6m square can be displayed (permission under Class 3[D]). Planning 'standard conditions' are that signs are clean, tidy, safe, permitted by the site owner, do not obscure transport signs, and can be removed carefully (from *Planning Portal*: bit.ly/2jLasyb). Religious institutions have 'deemed consent' for some permanent signs under class 2(c) in England and Wales, and 2(3) in Scotland and Northern Ireland. You may be limited to 1.2 square metres, and one on each road frontage.

Banners do not normally require a faculty or planning permission, provided they're not there for longer than one month before the event and two weeks after.

There is guidance for churches on the National Churches Trust site here: bit.ly/2kcYgou.

Church external signage providers

- CPO, www.cpo.org.uk—call 01903 263354 for a free consultation on what you want
- www.signconex.co.uk
- www.signsforchurches.co.uk
- www.churchnoticeboards.co.uk
- www.signomatic.co.uk

Large public signage

For an introduction to Out-of-Home advertising, try Exterion's guide here: bit.ly/2kd3Uqu.

Local companies often manage bus shelter and billboard advertising. One individual CPO customer in the south-west paid to display an outreach poster for two weeks before Easter for less than £250. You may need to get quotes from large companies such as Exterion, Signkick, Clear Channel Direct or Outdoor Advertising Ltd for your area.

UK church digital signage specialists

- www.apicommunications.co.uk
- www.a-a.uk.com
- www.spectra-displays.co.uk

Examples of words on noticeboards

- 'We seek to be a centre of attentiveness to the living God and a place of challenge and reconciliation.'
- 'We welcome you to our services and hope you will find us a home of generous hospitality.'
- 'We care and we'll share your problems. We listen—we do not judge. We accept you as you are.'
- 'Unified by love and hope, Jesus welcomes all. Worship Him here together.'
- 'Churches Together welcome you and invite you to join them for worship, refreshments and other activities.'
- 'Your local church welcomes you.'

To build a picture of the UK church

- www.greatcommission.co.uk from the Evangelical Alliance
- *Talking Jesus*: www.talkingjesus.org
- Bob Jackson, *What Makes Churches Grow?* (Church House Publishing, 2015)

To build a picture of your locality

- The Centre for Theology & Community has a list of sources of local information for churches, such as those mapping poverty or religious affiliation, with questions for churches to use: bit.ly/2l494XE
- Census summaries from www.neighbourhood. statistics.gov.uk/dissemination, or the incredible www.datashine.org.uk
- A free trial of Acorn (www.acorn.caci.co.uk) will describe your neighbours down to where they're likely to shop
- If you're brave enough to use a questionnaire to find out what people think of your church, sample questions might include:
  - How long have you lived in the area?
  - What local services do you use?
  - What are some of the issues locally?

- Have you ever connected with [name of church] in any way?
- Have you visited the church hall or equivalent?
- Did you know that the church offers [activity/event/course/service]?
- Would you find it useful to be notified of future courses/events?
- Would you like prayer?

Developing your building

- Start here: www.hrballiance.org.uk/resources/help-advice
- Roger Sutton, *How Churches Can Engage with Civic Society: 20 golden nuggets* (Gather, 2015), bit.ly/2jMovmk
- Germinate (Arthur Rank Centre) have excellent summaries, articles and links, relevant to all churches, not just rural ones: bit.ly/2l8n6o4
- National Churches Trust: bit.ly/2kcTapf
- Churches Conservation Trust guidance and case studies: bit.ly/2jBHX2q; and business plan toolkit: bit.ly/2iXScfO

Denomination specifics

- Church of England (but relevant to others): www. churchcare.co.uk
- Church of Scotland: bit.ly/2iXpo6W (range of leaflets) and bit.ly/2jjskMc (handbook)
- Church in Wales: bit.ly/2k0bHWx
- Roman Catholic Church in England and Wales: bit.ly/2iNT23m
- The Methodist Church: bit.ly/2jKCvg6
- The Baptist Union: bit.ly/2k0gZS7
- The United Reformed Church at time of writing no longer publishes its property handbook online, and suggests you contact your synod's property officer.

General buildings fundraising advice

- The Church of England's Parish Resources: www. parishresources.org.uk/resources-for-treasurers/ funding
- www.cuf.org.uk/near-neighbours/Resources
- The Institute of Fundraising has much useful material (including short videos providing a snapshot of the key principles of successful

fundraising): www.institute-of-fundraising.org.uk/guidance/introduction-to-fundraising

- Books by Maggie Durran are also excellent on this

On accessibility in churches for those with disabilities

- www.signsofgod.org.uk: a source for sign-language interpreters
- www.gosign.org.uk: Christian videos with sign language
- www.prospects.org.uk: focus on learning disabilities
- www.torchtrust.org: advice on the visually impaired
- www.disabilityandjesus.org.uk

There is also advice from Church Care (bit.ly/2qFofsl) and Germinate (go to www.germinate.net and search for 'accessibility').

On church art

- www.acetrust.org
- www.commission4mission.org
- www.christianartists.org.uk
- www.artandsacredplaces.org

Architects who think about mission

Some examples of UK church specialists:

- www.churchbuildingprojects.co.uk
- www.church-architects.co.uk
- www.cplarchitects.co.uk/portfolio.html

US church communications blogs

- www.sundaymag.tv/browse/communication
- www.beyondrelevance.com
- www.chuckscoggins.com/blog
- www.churchtechtoday.com
- www.churchmarketingsucks.com
- www.churchm.ag
- www.prochurchtools.com
- www.katieallred.com

UK church communications blogs

- www.churchtrain.uk
- www.premierdigital.org.uk
- www.samevine.co.uk/blog
- www.churchesaliveonline.com/blog
- www.cpo.org.uk/toolkit

Free images

- www.unsplash.com
- commons.wikimedia.org (make sure not to put 'www.' before this link)
- www.flickr.com/creativecommons
- Google: in Google Images, click 'Settings' at the bottom right, then 'Advanced Search'. Under 'Usage rights', choose those 'free to use or share'.
- www.photopin.com
- www.sitebuilderreport.com/stock-up
- www.churchm.ag/unsplashalternatives
- www.morguefile.com

Photo guidelines

A visual overview of church design layout can be found in the free download linked to the Grove booklet 'Publicity and the Local Church' by Nicola David: bit.ly/GrovePublicity.

You will also find advice and tools to create your own images here:

- pablo.buffer.com
- spark.adobe.com
- www.canva.com

Church logos

- www.cmsucks.us/n1
- www.churchlogogallery.com
- www.outreach.com/Church-Logos

Design brief questions

Answer these before commissioning a designer:

1. What is the goal of your project, in no more than two sentences?
2. Who is your target audience (for example, age, gender, worldview, location)?
3. Do you want them to do something specific as a result of the project (e.g. check a website)?
4. Do you have specific format requirements?
5. Where do you expect this to be seen?
6. How do you want people to feel when they see this?
7. Does it need to sit alongside or appear to be linked with any other design?
8. Do you have any samples of inspiration? Have you seen anything you'd like to build on?
9. Are there brand guidelines or an established look and feel that needs to be followed?
10. Can you nominate an individual to be responsible?

Data protection and church copyright

London Diocese's parish communications toolkit has up-to-date sections on copyright and on data: bitly.com/ParishCommsToolkit.

On data protection, churches are subject to the rules set out by www.ico.gov.uk. A helpful briefing for churches is at bitly.com/StewardshipData.

For advice on music, lyrics and video, contact CCLI (01323 436100; www.ccli.com).

Church videos

- Free training: www.prochurchtools.com/church-video-series
- 'Church video production for newbies': bit.ly/2kDWOMt
- 'The Best Royalty Free Production Music Sites': bit.ly/2jOEGLI

Outreach through community courses: examples

- Parenting: new-wine.org/resources/family-time
- Marriage/parenting: www.themarriagecourses.org
- Families: www.careforthefamily.org.uk/courses
- Divorce and separation recovery: www.restoredlives.org
- Money management and debt: bit.ly/CAPmoneycourse

For courses explicitly exploring Christianity and spiritual things, the website www.greatcommission.co.uk from the Evangelical Alliance enables you to search by emphasis, audience and seasons. You may also find www.disciplekit.org from CPAS helpful, with reviews of different resources.

Outreach to schools

- Ideas and advice from Scripture Union at bit.ly/2l9g9D2
- More about RE at www.barnabasinschools.org.uk, www.retoday.org.uk, www.request.org.uk, www.reonline.org.uk
- Bible Society storytelling volunteers: www.openthebook.net

- The amazing charity TLG links churches with vulnerable children and young people in school: www.tlg.org.uk
- Enabling creative prayer in schools: www.prayerspacesinschools.com

Consider going to the Hand in Hand conference in Eastbourne in February each year and, irrespective of which church you attend, find Church of England and Catholic education advisers and departments on social media.

All these links and more can be found at www.cpo.org.uk/toolkit.

Notes

1   Giles Fraser, *The Guardian*, 5 January 2016. The full article is worth a read: bit.ly/2kAQwKh.

2   Acts 16:13, 16.

3   Charles Spurgeon, 'The church—the world's hope', sermon preached at the Metropolitan Tabernacle, bit.ly/2kAZpaT.

4   Mark 12:31.

5   www.twitter.com/SlowChurches, 7 January 2016.

6   Bob Jackson and George Fisher, *Everybody Welcome* (Church House Publishing, 2015), p. 13.

7   Lesslie Newbigin, *The Gospel in a Pluralist Society* (Grand Rapids, MI: Eerdmans, 1989), p. 227.

8   Bob Jackson, *What Makes Churches Grow?* (Church House Publishing, 2015), pp. 129–30.

9   Paula Gooder, in *HOPE: Heartbeat of Mission* (Hope 08, 2013), p. 13.

10 Churches Trust for Cumbria, bit.ly/2k9yamL.

11 Churches Trust for Cumbria, bit.ly/2kAVV8p.

12 'Report from the Archbishops' Evangelism Task Group' (General Synod, 2016), p. 36, bit.ly/2kd2Ss1.

13 National Churches Trust, *The National Churches Trust Survey*, 2011, bit.ly/2iOu4Ba.

14 *Leading Your Church into Growth* workbook, p. 70.

15 Nicola James, *Publicity and the Local Church* (Grove Books, 2007), p. 5.

16 Examples at www.cpo.org.uk, including 'verse cards', and at www.preditos.com.

17 Pastor Agu Irukwu, Chair of the Executive Council, RCCG UK and Senior Pastor, Jesus House UK, quoted in *HOPE*, p. 6.

18 Some examples are www.churchbuildingprojects. co.uk, www.church-architects.co.uk, www. cplarchitects.co.uk/portfolio.html.

19 There is also an excellent downloadable commentary and summary produced by the Historic Religious Buildings Alliance, bit.ly/ HBAtoolkit.

20 Neil Pugmire, *100 Ways to Get Your Church Noticed* (Church House Publishing, 2014), p. 34.

21 Advice from www.commission4mission.org.

22 Church Care: bit.ly/2qFofsl; Germinate: bit. ly/2qFhgQJ.

23 www.london.anglican.org/kb/provision-for-people-with-disabilities.

24 Phillip Dawson, 'Enfield Deanery, Church Noticeboards', bit.ly/2jjQyu0.

25 Asendia, '5 reasons why direct mail is not dead', bit.ly/2jF6Fkq; Direct Marketing Association 'Direct Mail by Numbers', bit.ly/2kBCpFl.

26 Anne Coomes, *Your Church Magazine: how to make the most of it* (Parish Pump, 2007), p. 3, free to download at www.parishpump.co.uk.

27 www.renew37.co.uk.

28 Roger Sutton, *How Churches Can Engage with*

Civic Society: 20 golden nuggets (Gather, 2015), bit.
ly/2jMovmk.

29   www.healingonthestreets.com; www.amazon.
co.uk/Ultimate-Treasure-Hunt-Supernatural-
Evangelism/dp/0768426022.

30   Jules Middleton, 'Treasure Hunting Guidelines',
bit.ly/2js4soQ; includes a downloadable guide.

31   See *HOPE*.

32   www.passiontrust.org.

33   www.fusionyac.org/ocf/testimonials.php.

34   Simon English, 'He's an adman, not a madman', *The
Times*, 5 August 2016.

35   www.thereishope.co.uk/how-it-works/town-
city-use.

36   Pugmire, *100 Ways*, p. 29.

BRF

Transforming
lives and communities

Christian growth and understanding of the Bible

Resourcing individuals, groups and leaders in churches for their own
spiritual journey and for their ministry

Church outreach in the local community

Offering three programmes that churches are embracing
to great effect as they seek to engage
with their local communities
and transform lives

Teaching Christianity in primary schools

Working with children and teachers to explore Christianity creatively
and confidently

Children's and family ministry

Working with churches and families to explore Christianity creatively
and bring the Bible alive

Visit **brf.org.uk** for more information on BRF's work
Review this book on Twitter using **#BRFconnect**

brf.org.uk

The Bible Reading Fellowship (BRF) is a Registered Charity (No. 233280)